Mummy is taking me.
'It's a lovely day for a swim,' she says.

We arrive at the pool. I buy my own ticket.

We change into our swimsuits.
'We're going to the nursery pool,' says Mummy.

It's much bigger than my paddling pool.
A lifeguard sits by the edge to make sure everyone
is safe.

There are some children here already. Some of them are only little babies.

They are having a lovely time splashing in the water.

'Come on. Let's go into the water,' says Mummy.
It feels lovely and cool.

'Mummy, this water smells funny.'
'It has something in it to keep it clean,' Mummy explains.

The water isn't very deep.
'Lie on your tummy,' says Mummy. 'I'll hold you.
Don't be scared.'

Mummy pulls me along gently. I kick my feet.
Splash! Splosh! The water goes flying...

...all over a baby with her Daddy. She starts to cry.
'Don't cry, baby,' I say pulling a funny face.

Why isn't my Daddy here? I wonder.
'Will Daddy come next time?'

'Daddy can't swim,' says Mummy. 'Now, try floating on your back.'

Mummy holds me and we go to the middle of the pool. I can splash as much as I like here.

Now I turn over and paddle fast.
'Oh look Mummy. What's that monster over there!'

It isn't a monster after all, just a little girl with a
rubber ring.

Now we go to the side of the pool.
'Hold on to the bar,' says Mummy. She holds my
feet then gently lets me go.

'That's very good,' says Mummy. 'We'll soon have you swimming. But that's enough for today.'

We have a shower and change out of our swimsuits. I do feel clean. I won't need a bath for weeks and weeks!

Daddy is waiting for us outside.
'How was your first day at the swimming pool?'